THE SECRET
of STROMA

GW00727933

Written by Penny McKinlay
Illustrated by Gary Rees

Collins Educational
An imprint of HarperCollins*Publishers*

Chapter 1

It was a long hot summer's day, but then that was the way days always were at Gran's house.

Gran was shelling peas in the sun lounge at the back of the house. No-one shelled peas except for Gran. If it wasn't for seeing Gran shelling peas, Caroline would have always thought that they just came out of those green bags in the freezer.

Caroline sighed, a heigh-ho sigh heavy with happiness, and Gran smiled over at her. Caroline loved staying with Gran. No-one bothered her, no-one pestered her that it was time do this, time to do that. It was partly, of course, that time at Gran's house wasn't school time, it was holidays. But it was more than that. At Gran's it seemed that time stood still, that time was different. It was as if the memories Gran kept locked away, like odd bits and pieces in her chest of drawers, had escaped and left their heavy scent hanging in the air.

The air was so thick with memories, dancing in the motes of dust in the sunlight, you could almost stretch out and catch hold of them, pull them to you, make them your own. But not quite. They belonged to Gran.

It was special too, of course, because Caroline was on her own. Susan, her older sister, was too busy growing up to come to Gran's house now, too busy hanging about at home listening to pop music and being bored.

Susan was always going on about being thirteen. Being thirteen seemed to mean that you couldn't possibly be interested in all those things you had enjoyed so much one summer ago. Chiefly, it seemed to Caroline, it meant you suddenly became boring as well as bored, and if that's what growing up was all about then it would suit her to stay ten for the rest of her life.

Caroline stood up. "I'm just… " and then she stopped. Gran didn't need a minute-by-minute account of her plans: she could just go.

Gran smiled up at her. "See you at dinner time."

Caroline wandered back inside. Today was for the house. Yesterday, her first day, she had roamed the walled garden that surrounded the house.

Stroma had once been surrounded by other large Victorian houses, according to Gran, but they had been hit by a bomb in the war, and only Stroma had survived. New houses had been built on each side, but Stroma's high walls of warm red brick blocked them out as if they didn't exist.

At the bottom of the garden were the old ruined glass-houses, their skeletons rattling gently in the breeze, the glass long ago broken and taken away. Gran said that in the old days the gardener had to have a carnation blooming for a buttonhole for the gentleman of the house every day of the year, even when the snow was thick on the ground.

Caroline wandered happily through the house, soaking in the atmosphere and enjoying the coolness of the rooms with their high ceilings. In one room, she stopped and knelt in front of a glass-fronted cupboard full of tiny pieces of china – fairy-sized cups and saucers and little vases with delicate painted scenes etched round in gold. When she was small Caroline had always wanted to have dolls' tea parties with that miniature china. Now she could see why no-one else had thought it was such a good idea at the time.

Now Caroline was older, she and Gran would look at the exquisite china together, and Gran would tell her the story of each pretty cup and saucer, each little ornament. None of the pieces matched, Gran explained, because they had been gifts from different employers when she had been in service many years ago. Caroline didn't really

understand what Gran meant about being in service. It belonged to a far away time that was locked away, as firmly as those glass doors had been locked against her when she was three years old.

Sometimes, when Caroline asked her about the old days, Gran would talk about the grand parties, about sitting at the top of the stairs looking at the fine ladies and their glittering gowns. Caroline would drink it all in, imagining herself down there in the party, feeling the swish of silk as she danced away the night.

"I wish I'd been alive then," Caroline would say wistfully, and then a hard line would come to Gran's mouth and she'd lock away the pretty things once more. "We'll look again tomorrow," she'd say, pulling herself stiffly to her knees and hugging Caroline close to her. And when she released her, the hard line was gone and there was Gran's soft smile once more.

Caroline got up and went into the wide hall with its cold black and white tiles. She hesitated at the foot of the banisters and gazed up at the huge mirror at the turn of the stairs. It took up the whole of the wall, its heavy gold frame stretching up so high it made Caroline dizzy to look.

Close-up, the mirror was really rather shabby. It had lost much of its silvering, leaving misty patches that you could almost see through instead of seeing yourself looking back. It was as if it were stuck halfway in time, neither here nor there, neither now nor then. Dad said it was just old and needed re-silvering, but Caroline rather liked the way it wouldn't reflect the dull things it was shown nowadays. She quite liked having to fill in the missing bits of herself with her imagination.

Caroline moved on up the stairs and wandered into Gran's bedroom, with its huge dark wood chests and wardrobes. Gran had often shown Caroline the bits and pieces she kept in the deep drawers – soft shawls like cobwebs, lacy gloves, delicately embroidered handkerchiefs – but she still felt decidedly uncomfortable about looking at them on her own.

Despite her uneasy feelings, she did look, and even tried a shawl around her shoulders and pulled some long gloves up on her bare arms, her most unladylike summer suntan showing through the ivory lace. She showed her patchwork self, bright patches of tee shirt showing under the shawl, to one of the mirrors in the wardrobe. But then a new thought came to her, and she pranced halfway down the stairs to the great mirror.

That was much more satisfactory, for the old mirror obligingly seemed to blot out her modern bits and only showed soft lace. She reached out to touch the glass with her gloved hand – and gasped.

Her hand went straight through the mirror as if it were sinking into a mist.

Chapter 2

Caroline drew her hand back sharply, and looked around her, half-fearing and half-hoping that someone might have seen what had happened. Half-fearing, because surely putting your hand through a valuable old mirror was really rather naughty; half-hoping, because somebody would have been able to tell her whether she was imagining things. But of course no-one else had seen, so there was nothing for it but to try again.

Sure enough, her gloved hand melted through the mirror once more. Caroline waved it about, to see what it felt like on the other side. But there's only so much a hand can tell you, no matter how much you wave it about. It just felt like nothing.

Caroline drew her hand back again and thought.

Walking through a mirror into nothingness wasn't really very appealing. What if she just dissolved, never to be seen again? What if she couldn't get back again? But wait, perhaps if she just poked her head through, then she'd have the rest of her body left here to pull her back if she didn't like the look of whatever was on the other side.

Acting on this impulse, Caroline pushed her head into the mirror… and gave herself the most colossal crack against the glass. It hadn't worked – her head wouldn't go through.

Puzzled – and biting back tears from the bump – Caroline tried her hand again. It melted into the mist. She tried two hands. They both went through.

Caroline drew them back again and thought hard.
Why her hands but not her head? Then Caroline
thought of the gloves. Perhaps it was the gloves that
made the difference. Perhaps they were magic
gloves, like a conjuror's hat. But, not being a
conjuror's white rabbit, she could hardly get her
whole body inside the gloves, could she?

Caroline had another thought. She pulled the lace
shawl over her head and pushed her head, more
cautiously this time, towards the mirror.

This time there was no thud of hard head against
hard glass. Caroline's shawled head melted through
the silvered mist and at last she could see through to
the other side.

Standing there, with a feather duster in her hand,
was a young girl about the same age as Susan.
She was wearing a funny white cap and a long black
dress with a white apron, and her mouth was wide
open as if she was about to let out the most
enormous scream.

It was difficult to tell who was most surprised –
the girl at seeing a bodyless head poking through
what had seemed a perfectly normal mirror, or
Caroline, divided in half like a magician's assistant
when the trick had gone horribly wrong.

Caroline recovered first. "Don't scream. It's all
right. I know it must look pretty strange, that is, it is
pretty strange… "

But hearing the bodyless head talking was too
much for the girl and she started to back away,

opening and shutting her mouth like a stranded fish.

"Watch out!" Caroline shouted, and without thinking whether she could, or should, she launched her whole body out of the mirror and caught hold of the girl just as she was about to step backwards off the top of a flight of stairs.

Just in time, Caroline had worked out that what she was seeing was a mirror image of the house she had just left behind, that she had come out of the mirror at the same place she had gone into it, at the turn of the stairs.

The girl looked as though she would almost rather have fallen down the stairs. She shrank away from Caroline's arms, backing against the banisters, whimpering with fright.

"Who... what... how... did you?" she finally spluttered out.

"I don't know," replied Caroline – which would have answered almost any question put to her at that moment. She just about knew her name was Caroline, but as to where or when – or even how – she was, she really didn't know. But she felt she owed the girl some sort of explanation.

"I just came through the mirror," she said. "It kind of melted when I pushed against it."

Caroline felt she deserved something in return for this. "Who are you?"

"I'm..." The girl was about to reply when – "Jane!" A voice came sharply from below. "Where is that girl?"

Caroline shrank back into the shadows as a

woman dressed in the same uniform but with a neat, pretty lace collar, came to the foot of the stairs and looked up.

"There you are! Come back down here and look at this grate. If the mistress sees the way you've blacked it this morning you'll never keep your place here, and you'll be getting me into trouble along with yourself."

Jane – for Caroline presumed that must be her name – gave one last startled look at Caroline, clattered off down the stairs and disappeared through one of the doors off the hall.

Chapter 3

Left alone, Caroline debated whether to go upstairs or downstairs – "Or in my Lady's chamber," she giggled nervously to herself – for all this felt as real as a nursery rhyme or a fairy tale.

In the end she decided to go up, thinking that if Jane saw her again it might frighten her into a complete fit – in which case she probably wouldn't keep her 'place', if that meant job, as Caroline guessed.

Upstairs, Caroline's guess about this house being a mirror image of Gran's proved right. The rooms were just the same shape, the doors in the same place, but everywhere was darker and gloomier, with heavy curtains drawn against the sunlight. Caroline crept over to the windows, and peeped outside.

Another shock, for although Caroline had worked out the mirror-door had somehow taken her back in time, she was still startled by how different everything was outside.

There were no new houses crowding in on each side. The walled garden was there – much neater and better kept than Gran's garden – and at the bottom, the sun glinted on the panes of the glasshouses. Inside, Caroline thought she could make out the deep reds and pinks and whites of carnations in bloom. Over the high walls Caroline could see another large walled garden like Stroma's, presumably belonging to another house just like it.

Caroline turned back to the bedrooms once more, where everything seemed more familiar.

Certainly the toilet was the same, with the great old metal cistern high up on the wall. But the bathroom was quite different – apart from being extremely cold (how could anyone bear to take their clothes off?) it was dominated by a magnificent bath standing proudly on lion's paws.

By now Caroline thought it might be safe to explore downstairs, without bumping into anyone. She peered over the banisters to check that the coast was clear, and crept down.

The hall floor was the same as Gran's, black and white tiles, and the rooms were in the same place, but again much darker and gloomier than Gran's. No-one seemed to want to let the sunlight in. There was something very cold and unfriendly about the whole house, very different from the sunny, loving atmosphere of Gran's house. It made the house feel very unfamiliar, even though Caroline was sure by now this was Stroma.

In the gloom of the rooms downstairs, Caroline could make out heavy furniture, little tables each with its own lacy mat, glass cases containing grim-looking stuffed animals and birds, and ornaments and pictures everywhere. There was a massive mantelpiece with sides as heavy as an elephant's legs, bestriding a grate that looked very black indeed.

Seeing the grate reminded Caroline of the girl she had terrorised earlier. There was no sign of her now, nor of the older maid who had come to scold her. In fact, there was no sign of anyone in this cold, dark, unfamiliar house.

Feeling a bit frightened for the first time, Caroline went back into the hall and stopped, uncertain as to where to go next. Part of her had started to feel she'd quite like to go back home to Gran, but another, braver part of her wanted to carry on exploring.

As she hesitated, she suddenly heard the sound of voices, and before she'd worked out what was happening, the front door opened and a tall woman, wearing the sort of romantic dress Caroline had always dreamed of, swept in, calling behind her, "That will be all for today, Simons. You can put the car away."

Caroline just had time to creep under the hall table before the woman turned and came to stand right in front of it to unpin her hat in the mirror. Suddenly the hall, which only a few minutes ago had seemed so eerily quiet, was bustling with life. Another pair of feet came hurrying down the hall, which Caroline guessed belonged to the older maid. She must have bobbed a curtsey, for the black skirt crumpled down and then straightened again.

"Lunch will be served directly, ma'am," said the maid, and without a word of greeting or thanks, the tall woman swept away into the front room.

Caroline felt able to breathe again, and crept out from under the table. But just as she was

straightening up, she heard those swishing skirts again and saw the woman coming out of the room, heading for the stairs.

Caroline had had enough. She turned and ran up the stairs to the mirror, determined to escape from this strange world. Thinking quickly, she wrapped her shawl around her head and dived for the mirror. But once again came that agonising thump of forehead against thick glass. Panicking now, Caroline tried pushing her hands through, but to no avail. She banged her fists against the unyielding, shining surface in frustration, while behind her she heard the woman starting to mount the stairs.

She was stuck on the wrong side of the mirror.

Chapter 4

The mirror had failed her, but Caroline had to do something. The woman was still coming upstairs, and if Caroline stayed where she was, she could hardly avoid tripping over her.

So Caroline headed upstairs, and then panicked again. Where was the woman going? She could be heading for any of the bedrooms, even the toilet, if ghosts (were these ghosts?) went to the toilet. Then Caroline remembered the back stairs, leading to the attics, where Gran kept all the things she had never got round to throwing out.

She ran on tiptoe to the door which opened onto the back stairs and turned the handle as quietly as possible. Fortunately the hinges were better oiled than Gran kept them, and the loud squeak that Caroline had dreaded never came. Caroline crept through the door and closed it almost soundlessly behind her. She heard the woman's footsteps going into one of the bedrooms and let out a sigh of relief.

Caroline sank down on the stairs to think. Whichever way you looked at it, things weren't looking good. Here she was, stuck heaven knows how many years back in time, in a get-up that looked odd to put it mildly. A mixture of Marks and Spencer's best and brightest summer clothes and some bits of faded lace. She looked down at herself and smiled. Then she remembered the maid, Jane, and her complete amazement. You couldn't blame her for being struck dumb, thought Caroline. First she must have seen one hand wiggling and apparently waving at her through the mirror, then two hands, followed some minutes later (allowing for Caroline's thinking time) by a head. To be saved from falling down the stairs by a whole body suddenly jumping at her must have left her completely stunned.

What must she be thinking now? thought Caroline to herself, and giggled.

None of this, however, was helping her situation, she thought, feeling hopeless again. Unless… she looked down again at her patchwork outfit. She had got here by pushing through with bits of her body that were covered in old clothes. When she had tried to get her head through without being covered it hadn't worked. Maybe if she took off the old clothes, and pushed through with her modern shorts first? It would mean going bottom first, of course. But it would be a softer place to bump if her theory was wrong. She giggled again.

I must be getting light-headed, she thought to herself. All those bangs on the head and no lunch. Ah, well, it's worth a try.

So she inched open the door and peered round, listening to find out if the woman had gone back down for her lunch.

She hadn't. She suddenly came out of one of the bedrooms, having changed into a different dress. Caroline gasped and ducked back behind the door again, but the woman seemed not to have heard, and carried on down the stairs.

After waiting for a few moments, Caroline crept back to the banisters and peered over, remembering as she did so how Gran had described watching the grand parties from the top of the stairs. For the first time, Caroline felt a little of what Gran must have felt, always watching, never able to join in.

All was quiet in the hall below, so Caroline set off to try her experiment.

Taking the shawl and the gloves off and holding them, she backed into the mirror bottom first, hoping and praying that Gran wasn't standing on the other side watching a pair of red shorts coming through her mirror.

It worked. Instead of that sickening thump against hard glass, her bottom sank through the mist, leading the rest of her body after it. Even her hands which were holding the old clothes came through – Caroline had thought she might have to drop Gran's things on the other side if it came to a choice of them or her hands.

As her whole body came through the mirror in one piece, she heard Gran calling out, "Caroline, lunch is ready!"

Chapter 5

Caroline popped into Gran's bedroom to return the gloves and shawl and then raced down for lunch, wondering how long Gran had been calling her.

But it couldn't have been long, because lunch was still hot on the table, and Gran was just coming through carrying hers. It was the usual Gran lunch, two slices of meat and gravy, potatoes and, of course, those peas. You didn't get what Gran called that 'fancy foreign stew' or anything like that here – just plain meat or mince and plain vegetables, and always a pudding, not just a yoghurt or an apple like at home. Caroline liked food like that, and she was hungry, so she started to wolf it down.

"What did you find to do this morning?" asked Gran after a while, when she thought Caroline had eaten enough to be ready for a little conversation. "It isn't dull for you to be away from all your things at home?" she added anxiously.

Caroline broke off from her wolfing. "No, of course not, Gran. I love it here. There's so much to look at, so many rooms to explore." More than Gran knew about, certainly, she thought to herself – in fact twice as many.

She started to ask Gran about the house, all sorts of questions she'd never thought of before. How old was it? How long had Gran lived here?

Gran told her bits and pieces. She and Grandad had bought the house some years ago, when

Grandad had retired. Most people when they retired bought a nice little bungalow by the seaside or somewhere near their children, laughed Gran.

"We moved away from the family and bought an enormous old house miles away from everyone."

She laughed again. "They all thought I was mad, but I had my reasons. Partly it meant I could have my grandchildren to stay, once you all started arriving on the scene. And however could we all have a Christmas together without Stroma?"

Caroline remembered Mum nagging Gran to sell Stroma when Grandad had died three years ago. But Caroline knew that the house was important to Gran.

"But why this house, Gran? Why Stroma?"

Gran suddenly clammed up, those little hard lines appearing round her mouth again.

"I just saw it advertised and liked the look of it," she said shortly. "I used to live around here a long time ago and I fancied coming back."

Then she stood up and disappeared to the kitchen at the back of the house to fetch the pudding.

Caroline trailed after her into the huge kitchen, where the modern cooker, fridge and washing machine always looked out of place.

"How old is Stroma, Gran?" she persisted.

"It was built in Queen Victoria's days," Gran said, and added, when Caroline looked a bit blank – "it's about twenty years older than me, Caroline, and it's got as many creaks and cracks!"

They both laughed together and Caroline wrapped her arms around Gran's waist and hugged her.

"But it's a happy house, Gran," she said, remembering the cold, unhappy atmosphere of the other Stroma.

"Yes, Caroline, it is a happy house... " and Caroline heard her say almost to herself... "it is now, anyway."

It was steamed jam pudding for afters – something Caroline never had at home.

"Come out and get some fresh air this afternoon," Gran said, as they cleared away the plates.

So any thoughts Caroline had of creeping back through the mirror had to be abandoned for the time being, and part of her was quite relieved to spend the afternoon in the sunshine, tidying up the garden with Gran.

Chapter 6

By the next morning, however, Caroline's curiosity had got the better of her fears, and she was eager to go back through the mirror.

Now she felt she understood the secret that unlocked the mirror-door, she collected the gloves and shawl from Gran's bedroom and hung about at the top of the stairs to check that Gran wasn't anywhere around to witness her beloved granddaughter disappearing into thin air. Then she took a deep breath, like a high diver, and ducked her shawled head into the mirror.

The sickening thud she half-feared never came, and she melted through, this time just letting the top of her head and her eyes through, so she could duck back if anyone was coming.

No-one was there, so she pushed right through to the other side.

As soon as she was through, the cold hit her as if someone had opened the door of a freezer.

Back in Gran's house it was mid-summer, and although the house was cool, it was nothing like this bone-aching cold. It was like Christmas at Gran's before Mum insisted she had central heating put in, when you had to run between the rooms that had a fire, for fear of turning into an icicle on the way.

Pulling the shawl tighter around her, Caroline wondered which way to go, considering going back to get something warmer to wear. Then she half-heard a sound that caught at her and stopped her dead. She waited and it came again from upstairs, this time the unmistakable heart-lurching sound of sobbing.

Caroline hesitated, wondering whether she could really cheer up someone who was living so many years before her – especially dressed in this strange get-up. Unless, of course, they took her for a clown.

She could never bear people crying though – even her sister Susan, when she'd had a row with Mum and Dad, which seemed to happen a lot these days. Oddly enough, as Caroline got closer to the crying, it sounded more and more like Susan, and the sobs tugged even harder at Caroline's heart.

The sobs weren't coming from the first floor, where the main bedrooms were, but further up, through the attic door, which was half-open.

Caroline went up the back stairs, and looked in turn into each of the little boxrooms. There were three little rooms up there in the roof, and to Caroline's surprise they weren't full of old boxes, but each one was sparsely furnished with an iron bedstead and a chest of drawers with a jug and bowl, presumably for washing.

There on the bed in the second room lay the sobbing person. It was the maid, Jane, with her face plunged into the pillow, which was soaking up all but the occasional sob.

Caroline wasn't sure what to do now she was here. Last time she'd seen Jane she'd almost frightened her into a fit. How could she possibly comfort her? Before she could change her mind and creep away, however, Jane sat up and started taking deep gulps of air, like someone blowing up a balloon, obviously trying to stop herself from crying.

It was while she was mid-gulp that Jane spotted Caroline in the doorway. Stuck like that, mouth open and eyes bulging, Jane looked as if she might explode, like a character from a Tom and Jerry cartoon.

"You must breathe," said Caroline, going over towards the bed. She reached to touch her, then stopped as Jane shrank away, but finally, to Caroline's relief, let out the breath she was holding.

"At least I've shocked her so much she's stopped crying," thought Caroline, and wondered what to say next.

"We met before, didn't we?" she said, for want of anything better.

Jane nodded, and a leftover sob escaped.

"Are you all right?" Caroline asked, and then carried on because it seemed better to be saying something – anything – rather than nothing.

"Well, that's silly, obviously you're not all right because you're up here crying all on your own."

Then a sudden thought struck her.

"Hey, it's not because of me you're crying, is it? Is it because I frightened you yesterday?"

Jane looked bewildered, and for the first time managed to speak.

"That wasn't yesterday," she said. "It was last

summer, just after I started here. Nine months ago. I always wondered if you'd come again… "

It was Caroline's turn to be puzzled.

"So it's not summer here?" and then realised how cold she felt up here with no heating, in her shorts and tee shirt and the shawl.

"No, of course not, it's March… " said Jane, and then stopped, staring as if she'd only just noticed Caroline's bare legs.

"But why haven't you got any clothes on, just those, those… " words seemed to fail her – "those bloomers?"

"Bloomers?" Caroline looked down at her shorts and then at Jane's long skirts, and realised for the first time that, to Jane, she must look as though she'd only got her knickers on. She blushed a little, feeling almost naked, and tried to rearrange the shawl – but there are limits to how far a shawl can stretch.

"Where I came from, on the other side of the mirror, it's summer," she started to explain – but there was so much to explain. "It's still summer, and it was only yesterday that I came before… and… it's years and years later than it is now for you… that is, years in the future, I suppose."

She trailed off, for Jane was looking lost.

"So you came through the mirror from a different time?" Jane wondered.

"Yes, but it's the same house," Caroline said. "I'm on holiday there with my Gran, and these are the sort of clothes we wear on holiday now – I mean then, in the future, that is," she added.

Jane looked disapproving, like Mum when Susan put on too much make-up.

"Well, they're a perfect disgrace," she said stuffily.

Caroline bristled. "They might not be right for weather like this, but those skirts can't be much use for climbing trees or playing outside when you are on holiday."

At the word holiday Jane started sobbing again.

"What's the matter?" cried Caroline. "Why are you so upset?"

Jane blurted out between sobs. "What use is a holiday if I'm stuck here, miles from my mother and Hettie?" she sobbed.

Caroline tried to understand. "So you've got a holiday, but you can't go and see them?" she said.

"That's right," said Jane, calming down a little and wiping her face with a hanky. "It's Mothering Sunday and everyone goes home to see their mother. We all get a day off... they've all gone, except me."

"But why haven't you gone too?" asked Caroline. "Couldn't someone give you a lift?"

Jane looked blank.

"In the car, I mean," Caroline added quickly.

"In the car?" Jane looked at her as though she were mad. "Oh, no, the car's just for the master and the mistress – why would they let me have the use of it, like a fine lady?"

She saw that Caroline didn't understand the problem at all.

"No, you see, I have to go on the train because it's quite a long way to get home, and I haven't the money. I haven't been here long enough to save up for the fare yet."

"But this is a job, isn't it?" Caroline said. "Surely you get money for working here?"

"Yes, but I send most of it home," said Jane. "They need the money with Father gone, and with me being the eldest. That's why I had to come away so far to work. It was a better position than I could have got closer to home."

"So you haven't been home since you came here last summer," said Caroline. "Not even for Christmas?"

Jane shook her head miserably, and looked as though she was about to start crying again.

Caroline's sense of justice was outraged by Jane's story. It was simply not fair, any of it, and she felt it was up to her to do something about it.

Then she suddenly remembered something. "I've got some money," she cried, and fished out of her pocket the money Dad had given her for the holiday.

"Five pounds," she said, a bit sadly because she'd had all sorts of plans for the money.

"Five pounds!" Jane almost choked. "But that's an awful lot of money! I don't need anything like that much to get to Mother's."

Her whole face lit up and when she smiled Caroline was again reminded of someone – Susan perhaps? She looked happy for the first time since

Caroline had met her.

"If I hurry and go now I could still get the train and be there by lunch time. Oh, what a surprise it will be for them!"

She started to think what she needed to take with her. Caroline held out the five pound note to her. But when Jane saw it the happiness faded from her face as fast as it had appeared.

"But that's not real money," she cried angrily, as if Caroline had been playing a cruel trick on her. "It's just pretend money, some silly child's game!"

She pushed Caroline away from her in a fury of disappointment and buried herself once more in the pillow, crying, "Get out, go away, leave me alone!"

Chapter 7

Caroline, now furious herself, stormed out of the attic room and would have slammed the door if she'd felt a bit more at home.

She felt like crying too, partly at the injustice of Jane's accusation, and partly because Jane had dismissed her as a 'child' – just as Susan did all the time nowadays.

Partly, though, it was because she could see how cruel it was for Jane one minute to think she was going to have the chance to go home, after dreaming of it for nearly a year – only to have it snatched away the next. It was like Cinderella's fairy godmother getting Cinderella all ready for the ball and then undoing it all with one wave of her magic wand and the words, "Sorry, just kidding!"

Although Caroline knew it wasn't her fault, she couldn't help feeling guilty – and feeling guilty made her feel even angrier, because she couldn't really blame Jane for hating her. However, by the time she had stormed to the foot of the attic stairs, she had calmed down and was left feeling very sorry for Jane.

She sat down on the bottom attic stair to think.

Perhaps there was some money in the house she could find and give to Jane. After all, her mistress obviously didn't pay her enough.

That idea didn't really appeal to her though. Something told her it wasn't right to take their money – and besides, Jane would probably get the blame for stealing and get the sack and maybe be thrown into prison for the rest of her life. Caroline didn't have much idea what the punishment would be for stealing – except she remembered from history lessons that at one time people were hung for stealing sheep.

The truth was, Caroline thought, she just didn't know how anything worked all these years before she was due to be born. If she was in her own time she could borrow some more money from Mum and do some jobs to pay it back, or else she could take some money out of her post office book.

The trouble was, this wasn't her own time. Unless… maybe… if she took Jane into her time, back through the mirror with her? She knew how to get to the town that Jane had talked about – she had seen the station on the way to Gran's. It was only about half an hour on the fast train.

Caroline raced back upstairs to Jane.

"Listen, why don't you come with me, back through the mirror, and we'll go on the train in my time – then we can use my money and it will be all right. Then we can go to your mum's house together… "

Then Caroline stopped, and went red at her own stupidity. Jane would be in the wrong time, she wouldn't be able to see her family. It would be pointless.

"Oh, but of course, your mum won't be there, she'll be… " she was going to say "dead" but realised how tactless that would be.

Instead of shouting at her again, as Caroline had expected, Jane looked interested.

"You mean, I could go through to your time, and find out what it's like, see into the future?"

Jane became quite excited, and Caroline realised with surprise that this maid, who up till now she'd only ever seen weeping and creeping around like a mouse, was at bottom a young girl who liked adventures, like her. It was just that she didn't get much chance to have them – her life was so adult and serious.

"It would be all right," said Jane, as if talking out loud to herself. "Nobody would miss me… Grace and Cook are gone for the day and the master and the mistress are out too, what with no-one being here to see to them."

She looked straight at Caroline and smiled, chasing away all trace of tears. "Yes! Let's go! You can take me on the train to see my home – it will be such fun!"

She laughed, and then added, "But I'm not wearing those bloomer things!"

Caroline had to think quickly. She hadn't considered how she was going to get Jane through the mirror, but she couldn't let her down now. Jane would have to borrow something of hers to get through, that was certain, but what? All she had on, apart from the shawl and the gloves, was a pair of red shorts, a blue tee shirt, white socks and trainers.

"Well, you'll have to wear something of mine to

get through the mirror," she said, and explained how the mirror worked.

In the end they settled for trying Caroline's trainers on Jane's feet, and off they went downstairs together to the mirror.

Jane was starting to look a little panicky, as though she might back down at the last minute. So, in spite of her own doubts, Caroline grasped her hand firmly, and backed through the mirror bottom first, half-dragging Jane behind her.

As she went through she yelled to Jane, "Remember, feet first!" and then she was through apart from her hands, which were still holding on to Jane's. She watched anxiously until she saw her own trainers appear, like someone surfacing feet first from a shining pool, followed by Jane's long black skirt.

She relaxed and smiled reassuringly as Jane's white face appeared. But then, as the last bits of Jane slipped through the faded silvering, there came the most deafening bang and the old mirror was rent by a jagged crack, like a streak of lightening, from top to bottom.

Chapter 8

The sudden sound made both girls jump and, for a few moments, they clung together like sisters seeking comfort.

Now that they were on her side of the mirror, in her time, Caroline felt responsible for Jane. Although she was younger than Jane, Caroline knew that she had to protect her, and take the lead. So although she was secretly horrified by the crack in the mirror, and terrified by what it might mean, she was the first to recover from the shock and started to reassure Jane.

"Don't worry, it doesn't matter. It's such an old mirror nobody will mind," she said.

In her excitement and bewilderment at being on the other side of the mirror, Jane simply accepted what Caroline said.

Caroline hurried her up the stairs to her room to find more suitable clothes for her to wear, but all the time she was sick with worry about what had happened. She didn't believe for one moment what she had said about nobody minding about the crack in the mirror. A mirror that size must cost a fortune to replace, certainly more than her holiday money, which she was about to spend on Jane in any case.

It wasn't just that, though. Would the magic of the mirror work with that great crack in it? Caroline tried to tell herself it would, but in her heart of hearts she didn't believe it. The mirror must have

cracked because they had broken the rules by travelling together across time. And her greatest fear, which she simply couldn't bring herself to share with Jane, was that Jane was stuck forever in the wrong time.

What had started out as an adventure to cheer Jane up had turned into a disaster. Jane would never see her mother or sister again now, unless they could find another way back. And how on earth was Caroline going to explain having suddenly acquired a teenage girl from thin air, with no home to go to? It wasn't exactly like secretly buying a pet hamster and keeping it hidden in her bedroom, as she had done last year. Jane was going to need food, somewhere to sleep...

Caroline's head was buzzing with all these fears, so she decided to ignore them, and pretend that everything was fine.

So she showed Jane her room and her things, and actually started to enjoy watching Jane's face, amazed by the most everyday things – the electric hairdryer which she kept turning on and off; the bright colours of the bedcovers and curtains Gran had bought for the room.

She was less impressed by the modern clothes and even laughed at them, which rather offended Carline. Jane couldn't believe that Caroline really only wore shorts and tee shirts most of the time, and she handled Caroline's favourite battered old jeans almost with disgust.

"They're like the gardener's overalls," she said.

"How can you wear these?"

Caroline felt even crosser, because she had been going to suggest that Jane borrowed them – she quite obviously couldn't go prancing around in that black dress. People would think she'd been to a funeral and or to a fancy dress party as a witch.

She dug around in a wardrobe and found a skirt and blouse Mum had insisted she bring in case Gran had wanted to take her somewhere smart. They were a bit crumpled – she supposed she should have hung them up – but Jane seemed to be happy with them, so she left her to get changed, since she didn't seem to want her to watch.

As Caroline left the room she sneaked a glance back, and burst into fits of giggles at the sight of Jane's long underwear. She could see why Jane was shocked by her clothes – her knickers were bigger than Caroline's shorts!

She was amazed – and pleased – when Jane threw one of her trainers at her to stop her from giggling. As she went off downstairs, she thought that perhaps the day wouldn't be such an ordeal. Now that Jane was relaxing a bit they might have fun together, even become friends. On this side of the mirror Jane wasn't so grown up, there was less of a gap between them.

At that, a sudden thought struck Caroline and she ducked her head back into the room, making Jane jump in surprise.

"By the way," she said. "How old are you?"

"Thirteen," said Jane.

"Just wondered," said Caroline. "I'm ten," she added, and then went off downstairs, struck by the difference in their lives. Jane was the same age as Susan, yet she had been sent to work miles away from home, with no holidays, no friends and presumably no school.

She wandered into the garden to find Gran, trying to look casual, but guiltily remembering the cracked mirror. She couldn't tell Gran now, though, she'd have to face that one later, once she'd kept her promise to Jane, if it was possible.

"I thought I might go for a picnic, Gran," she said when she found her, picking sweet peas for the house. "You haven't started lunch yet?" she added anxiously.

"No, not yet, dear. That's fine – just help yourself from the fridge. There's plenty of cheese and ham and bread, and take an apple with you... "

Caroline was already disappearing into the house.

She packed up the food quickly and shoved it into a carrier bag. When Gran came to look later she thought Caroline must have been very hungry, she seemed to have taken double what she'd normally eat. Being Gran, though, she just shrugged, and thought no more about it.

Caroline dashed back upstairs. Jane was dressed in her skirt and blouse and obviously felt a bit strange, but Caroline reassured her.

"You look fine," she said, and went on, "we ought to hurry, you know, if you want to see your house. I'm not sure when the next train leaves."

She found another plastic bag for Jane's clothes – they would need them if they found a way to get Jane back to her own time. She shoved in the shawl and gloves for herself, just in case. Then they hurried off downstairs and across the hall.

Just as Caroline opened the front door she heard Gran's voice behind her. Caroline froze, with a sick lurch in her stomach.

"What about a kiss goodbye, Caroline?" said Gran.

"Of course, Gran," she turned back and smiled at her. Then she added, as casually as she could, "Gran, this is Jane from down the road – she's coming on the picnic with me. Jane – this is my Gran, who I told you about."

Gran gave her the oddest look, without even glancing at Jane. Then Caroline heard Jane and Gran say, as if with one voice, "But there's no-one there."

There was a horrible pause, while Caroline just didn't know what to say. Jane was looking very panicky again, presumably at the idea that she could neither see other people nor be seen by them – she must be feeling like a ghost, thought Caroline.

Then Gran laughed, although still looking at Caroline a little oddly, and said, "You're a bit old to be bringing back your imaginary friend, aren't you Caroline?"

Caroline felt able to laugh then too, and Gran gave her a hug and sent her – and Jane, although she didn't know it – off through the front door into the bright sunshine.

Chapter 9

Caroline hurried Jane down the road towards the railway station, anxious not to miss a train, since it was already mid-morning. Jane, however, just wouldn't be hurried. She wandered along the road like a goldfish out of its bowl, wide-eyed and open-mouthed at everything she saw, especially the cars everywhere.

The odd thing was that although, like Gran, other people didn't seem able to see Jane and looked straight through her, Jane could see them, and stared quite rudely at their clothes as they passed. It was just Gran she hadn't been able to see. Caroline couldn't understand it, but she didn't get much chance to puzzle it out.

Jane was full of questions, and hardly seemed able to understand the answers Caroline gave her. Ordinary families having cars? Street lights that came on at night without someone coming to light them?

She wanted to know what had happened to the other houses like Stroma – why had these new houses been built? Caroline felt funny about telling Jane about the war that for her was still to come, that she would have to live through, and the terrible bombs that had destroyed the houses next to Stroma. So Caroline just fudged her answer, said that people liked these new houses better, because they were smaller and easier to look after. As she talked she started to understand things better herself – that now people didn't have servants they didn't need so many rooms.

"No servants?" Jane really seemed unable to believe this.

"How do people manage?"

"I suppose they just do it all themselves," replied Caroline, who'd never really thought. "There are lots of machines for things now – like washing machines, and vacuum cleaners to clean the carpets, and stuff… "

She trailed off as a woman passed by staring at her and she realised she must look like a lunatic talking to herself. She was quite glad of an excuse to stop Jane's questions for a bit.

"I can't talk when there are people around," she hissed. "They all think I'm mad."

So they walked in silence down to the station, Jane obviously itching to ask more questions.

When they got to the ticket office, Caroline realised with delight the advantages of Jane being invisible. Invisible people don't need tickets – which meant Caroline didn't have to spend all her holiday money on a ticket for Jane.

She asked for her ticket with as much confidence as she could muster, for Mum or Dad had always been with her to buy her ticket to come to Gran's. In fact this holiday was the first time she'd been allowed to come on the train alone.

The man told her the next train was due in five minutes, so together she and Jane went onto the platform to wait. Feeling very daring, she bought two Mars Bars with some of the money she had left. She was showing off by now to Jane, who made a great audience, as she was amazed at everything, especially Caroline having money to spend on luxuries like sweets.

The station, and even the train itself, seemed less of a novelty to her, although she was surprised there was no steam coming from the engine.

Once they were settled in seats some way from everyone else, Caroline handed Jane her Mars Bar and watched, giggling inwardly, as Jane chewed her way through it, silenced by its stickiness.

When they started talking again, they found themselves swapping notes about their lives, instead of Jane just asking Caroline questions. Jane told Caroline about her day – getting up before six to light the fires and get breakfast ready for the master before he went out to work; then the morning spent cleaning – really hard cleaning, brushing carpets, polishing all those fiddly ornaments and heavy furniture, blacking the dreaded grates… the list went on forever.

Caroline thought sheepishly how she and Susan moaned about taking their turns with the washing up, or the vacuuming, and what a hard time they gave Mum about getting up for school.

She asked Jane why she didn't go to school any more.

"What, at my age?" said Jane, a bit pompously. Then she added, with pride a little mixed with regret, "I finished school when I was twelve."

She'd got a job in a shop close to home, but then this situation came up that paid more "…so I had to come away and leave Mother and Hettie. The last time I saw them was when I waved goodbye to them at the station."

The tears came back to Jane's eyes, and she fell silent, looking out of the window.

Caroline was reminded of all the problems she had tried to put out of her head.

"You do know that we might not be able to find your old house, don't you? That it might be gone? And we almost definitely won't be able to get back to see your family this way… " and she mentally added, or any other way, since the mirror is cracked.

Jane smiled, and shook off her sorrows like a dog coming out of a muddy stream.

"Let's worry about that later, it's enough to be seeing all of this," she said.

Caroline got the food out of the carrier bag for their picnic. Even the fact that the cheese was wrapped in plastic and the bread was already cut into perfect slices was a source of wonder for Jane. She'd never seen crisps before, and spent ages examining what seemed to Caroline a perfectly ordinary plastic packet. Caroline might have been a magician unpacking his box of tricks for the pleasure it gave Jane.

While they were eating, Caroline didn't notice a boy of about eight wandering over and watching them eat. Or rather, he was watching Caroline eat, while in the space next to her, he could see food floating up from the bag and then quite suddenly disappearing into thin air.

Caroline saw him too late to warn Jane to stop eating.

"Well, boy," she said in her haughtiest tones. "What is it?"

"It's those butties," gasped the boy, "they're flying."

"Yes, boy, I am a witch, and those butties, as you put it, are enchanted butties. They are being eaten by a beautiful princess whom I have made invisible as a punishment for asking too many questions. If you ask me any more questions or tell anyone else about what you have seen I shall have to make you invisible too."

Then she saw that Jane was giggling and had drawn out a hatpin from the pocket of her dress in the bag.

"The first sign that you are becoming invisible is a sharp prick in your leg," said Caroline, picking up on Jane's plan. At this, Jane gave the boy's leg a gentle jab with the pin. He gasped and backed away down the train, rubbing his leg.

"Remember, not a word or you'll disappear," hissed Caroline after him, and he broke into a run back to his mother.

At that point, before his mother could come and demand an explanation, Caroline saw they were arriving at their destination. She stuffed the food back in the bag, and the pair of them fled from the train, laughing helplessly.

Chapter 10

The girls wandered around the town centre aimlessly for a while – and for both of them it was a relief to forget why they were here. Caroline could almost convince herself that it was she and Susan wandering around the streets together, good friends as they always had been until recently.

For Jane, the shop windows were a source of endless wonder, like a fairy grotto. There were so many things for sale that she had never even heard of, certainly never felt the need for.

Everywhere looked so different to her and yet, when she looked up, many of the buildings were the same. It was like seeing old friends in gaudy fancy dress and being taken in by their disguise until you glimpsed their faces underneath. This was the same town of black and white beams and weathered stone in which she had grown up – it had just been plastered over by modern shop fronts in brightly coloured plastic and huge neon letters, and gutted by gaping display windows.

The shop Jane was most fascinated by, to Caroline's amazement, was a toy shop. It seemed strange that Jane, whose life to Caroline was so horribly adult, with nothing but worry about work and money, was still interested in toys.

She jumped, and Caroline laughed, when a shop assistant pulled a cord in the back of a pretty doll with long blond hair, and the doll talked. Jane looked at Caroline almost fearfully, as if she'd brought her to a witch's cavern and she expected next moment to be turned into a toad.

Caroline still had a little of her holiday money left, so she left Jane watching some children playing with an electric car and searched the shop for a present for her. She settled on a tiny doll, wearing shorts and a tee-shirt, which was all she could really afford.

She was afraid that, after all, Jane might think the doll was childish, but she hugged Caroline with real delight, laughing at Caroline's choice of clothes for the doll.

Jane put the doll into the pocket of the skirt she was wearing. It reminded Caroline why they were really here. They couldn't put it off any longer.

"Look, you ought to change your clothes back again," she said to Jane. "No-one can see you anyway, and if we find a way back to your time you'll need to be wearing your own things."

She couldn't see why Jane couldn't just change her clothes there and then in the street, but Jane was horrified at the thought of stripping off in public.

"But no-one can see you, don't be so silly. It can't be rude to get undressed if you're invisible," Caroline argued.

Jane refused to give in. "I can't strip down to my underwear in the middle of the street, it's just not right. What if I suddenly reappeared, in front of all those people?"

In the end they wasted more time finding a

department store with changing rooms, and Caroline stood there waiting for Jane with mounting impatience, her irritation fuelled by her real worries about what was going to happen next. How could she possibly find a way of getting Jane back to her own time? All she could think of was another mirror − after all she could hardly describe herself as an expert on time-travel after one accidental stumble back in time.

Her mood was lifted a little by seeing another shopper pulling back the curtain to Jane's cubicle and walking in to try on a dress, blissfully unaware that an invisible but very embarrassed teenager was still changing inside. She hoped Jane wouldn't resort to the hatpin.

At last Jane reappeared, and the pair of them set off to see if Jane's house was even still standing − with an awful knowledge in Caroline's heart that this was Jane's only hope of returning to her proper time.

Chapter 11

It seemed strange to Caroline, after taking the lead since Jane had joined her in her own time, that in her own town it was now Jane who led the way. Even all these years later the layout of the streets was the same, and she set off confidently towards her old home.

Caroline felt a bit better when she saw how much of the town was still as Jane had known it – she had never really thought about the age of the buildings she saw before.

Both girls were getting increasingly nervous, however, and although they'd been chatting happily while they'd been looking round the shops, they now fell silent.

The silence was only broken when Jane suddenly said, "It's round this corner. It's the next street."

Neither could even look at the other.

They stopped on the corner.

In the end it was Jane who said, "Come on, we've got to see now we're here."

Together they turned the corner but Caroline was hanging back, hardly able to look. She heard Jane gasp – with relief or bitter disappointment she could hardly tell.

Then, "It's still there," Jane cried. "Over there – number ten – the whole street's still here… look!"

Caroline looked, and saw a row of low houses of reddish brick, much smaller than Stroma, which at one time must have been identical to one another. Now the line of the terrace was interrupted by a fancy window here, a grand front door there, and some houses had been painted in various colours, covering the brick beneath. It was like a photograph cut into jigsaw pieces, some in black and white and some in colour. Some of the little houses seemed stuck in time, whilst their brightly coloured neighbours had moved on.

"Which one is it?" she asked, terrified that Jane's old home would be one of those that had been modernised, gutted of all its memories – and its doors to the past.

"There," said Jane, and pointed again. "It's just the same!"

Caroline looked, and saw that she must be right.

Number ten was the same as it must have been all those years ago, looking blissfully battered and tumble-down, quite plainly untouched by all these 'improvements'.

Jane was pulling Caroline across the street, as if she had forgotten in her excitement that she was still out of her own time. It was almost as if Jane expected to knock on the door and to find herself wrapped in the warm embrace of her mother and sister.

Caroline ached inside for her, but she knew she had to shatter her happiness by bringing her back to here and now – instead of here and then.

"They're not there any more, you know," she said, almost roughly. "They've gone. It'll be different people there now, you won't know them."

She knew from the pain on Jane's face that she had been right about her thoughts.

She saw the pain replaced by anger; Jane looked for a moment as though she wanted to hit Caroline for bringing her back to reality. Then the angry look was gone. The excited, happy Jane who had tugged at her arm was replaced by the sad, submissive servant that Caroline had first met at Stroma.

"What shall we do then?" Jane said quietly. "Perhaps we'd better go back. I'll be missed if I'm not back for supper."

The gloom of her real life seemed to settle on to her again. To Caroline it was like hearing the song of a caged bird suddenly silenced by a dark cover placed on its cage.

"No, we're going to try and send you home to your family," said Caroline, stung by her pity into action. "There must be a chance, at least the house looks as though it hasn't changed much. Now think. Was there a mirror anywhere, maybe in the bathroom?"

Jane gave a half laugh. "Why, we haven't got a bathroom – just the toilet outside. It's only grand houses like Stroma that have bathrooms… "

Then she thought.

"There is – or was – " she corrected herself, "a big mirror upstairs, on the wall in Mother's room. Not like that one at Stroma, of course, nothing so fine, but one with a good frame that Mother had from her mother. She was proud of that mirror."

She sighed, "But it'll be long gone now, Caroline. Let's go back, I don't want to see any more."

Caroline knew that Jane was saying she didn't want to hurt any more, that for her the adventure had turned sour. Caroline felt she had to try, though, that they couldn't give up now.

"Well, there's a chance then. If the mirror was a good one, it will have been kept."

She was thinking of a plan quickly, for she knew that Jane was on the point of walking away.

"I'm going to knock and ask if I can use the toilet – there's bound to be a bathroom by now, even if there wasn't when you lived here, and that'll give me an excuse to go upstairs. Come on."

Caroline led the way firmly across the street to number ten and knocked on the door.

Chapter 12

The door was opened by a young man in dirty blue overalls, with dust and bits of plaster all over him.

"A'right, love?" he said cheerfully.

His friendliness made Caroline less nervous.

"I was wondering, could I use your bathroom?" Then she added, without knowing where the words were coming from, "You see, my gran used to live in this street when she was a girl and so I came to look, but I didn't know anyone here and I needed to go to the loo… " she trailed off.

She was conscious that Jane was staring at her, as surprised by her invention as Caroline herself. And yet Caroline didn't feel as guilty as if she'd told a lie; somehow it felt right, like suddenly seeing the answer to a sum that had puzzled her for ages.

The man was also staring at her, surprised and doubtful. He peered behind her into the street, "You all on your own, love?"

Caroline blushed, suddenly realising the danger she might have put herself in. She had forgotten that, as far as anyone else was concerned, she was totally alone.

"Yes… " she trailed off.

"You shouldn't go round knocking on strange doors. You never know who you might find." Then he laughed, "Never mind, love, just don't do it again. The toilet's upstairs. It won't be there much longer, we're ripping everything out upstairs."

Caroline's stomach gave a great lurch. What if they were just too late?

The man was still chatting as he showed her in.

"In a terrible state, this place, never bin touched, 'part from having a bathroom put in. Looks like it used to be a bedroom in the old days. Watch out for the plaster on the floor. I'll be out the back."

Caroline went gingerly up the bare wooden stairs, which were covered in the same fine dust. She looked back at Jane following her. Her face was constantly changing as different feelings flitted across it. Now delighted by a patch of familiar flowered paper exposed by the workmen; now desolate at the empty rooms with no echo of those she loved. She was bewildered by the ruin of her old home.

As they reached the top of the stairs, Caroline could almost feel Jane's excitement behind her, like a small snapping dog at her heels. They saw the bathroom instantly.

"He's right," Jane whispered – forgetting the builder could neither see nor hear her. "This was Mother's room."

This was it then, thought Caroline grimly. Their only chance.

She went through the door and scanned the room. And scanned it again, with her stomach lurching so violently she thought she would be sick. The only mirror was a small square one on the front of the bathroom cabinet. Even someone as new to time-travel as she could tell that mirror would take you nowhere. It was modern, it had no links with the past, no images of faces long gone locked away beneath its silvering. Apart from anything else, it was too small – you couldn't even get your head through.

Not knowing what to do next, Caroline closed the door and perched on the edge of the bath with Jane beside her, neither able to look at each other in their bitter disappointment.

As she was sitting there, Caroline glanced round the walls once again. Something on the wall caught her eye. A ragged-edged triangle of paper had been peeled away to reveal hardboard underneath. There was a hole where the hardboard had been broken and, as Caroline bent closer, there came an unmistakable silvery gleam, like a moonbeam escaping from the clouds on a stormy night.

She gasped with excitement and, beckoning Jane over, started pulling at the hole in the hardboard to make it bigger. Without thinking what anyone might say, together they wrenched at it with their bare hands, and gradually more and more silver shone through. When at last they found an edge with a simple smooth wooden frame, the polished finish dulled by neglect, Jane half-sobbed in disbelief, "It is, it's Mother's mirror."

The lower half of the hardboard over the mirror was covered in tiles – clearly the mirror had been boarded over so that the tiles could be laid over it.

It was much harder for the girls to pull away the tiled hardboard, but at last its own weight pulled it down, and Caroline caught the whole thing as it fell to the ground, narrowly avoiding a telltale crash.

There stood the whole mirror revealed, nothing like as magnificent as the Stroma mirror, but still lent an air of mystery by the weathering of time. The silvering on this mirror was faded too, so that the reflection of their white, strained faces came and went in patches, one moment there, the next vanished. And, for the first time since that awful crack sounded back at Stroma, Caroline allowed herself to believe there might be a way back for Jane.

The girls stared at each other. For Jane the mirror offered the hope of seeing her mother and sister for the first time in nearly a year; for Caroline the mirror offered the only hope that Jane would ever see them again.

Caroline broke the silence. When she first spoke her voice seemed to stick in her dry throat. She swallowed and tried again.

"Go on then, you'll have to just try."

She went on, trying to make light of it, and knowing as she spoke she was lying, "The worst that can happen is that you'll get a bump like I did."

Jane looked at her, startled.

"Aren't you coming, too?" she asked.

But for the first time Caroline's courage had failed. She simply couldn't face any more fear, any more of the terrible uncertainty she had been living with since the Stroma mirror cracked. And she knew, if she was right, they couldn't both go through the mirror, even if it did work, without it cracking. That would be asking too much again. And if both mirrors were cracked, she would be stuck in Jane's time just as Jane could still be stuck in her time.

She couldn't share all these fears with Jane, so she searched for a more practical excuse.

"I can't, I'm running out of time to get back to Gran's. She'll worry if I'm gone all day. Besides, those workmen are going to wonder what I am doing in here if I take much longer. They'll think I'm helping them redecorate!"

The girls giggled together. "For the last time," thought Caroline, half-sorry and half-hoping it was true.

"Go on," she said, pushing Jane towards the

mirror. Jane stretched out her hands to touch it. Nothing happened – just cold, hard glass.

"No, you'll have to go backwards," said Caroline impatiently. "It's your clothes that need to go through first."

Jane turned, and with her tense eyes fixed on Caroline's, she backed into the mirror. Closer and closer and then... yes... she was melting through, disappearing bit by bit like Alice's Cheshire Cat.

"Goodbye, Caroline," she whispered.

"Goodbye, Jane," Caroline whispered back.

Jane stopped, halfway home.

"I never told you, Caroline," she said quietly. "My name isn't really Jane. That's just what the mistress called me. She said she couldn't be bothered learning another maid's name. My name is Esther, really."

Then she melted away completely with a last goodbye, and Caroline sank back stunned onto the toilet, the closest thing she could find to sit on. For now she knew for certain what she had half known before – that Jane was her grandmother. For Esther was Gran's name.

Chapter 13

Caroline sat there for several minutes before she realised that the workmen must be wondering what she was doing in there.

So she crept down the stairs – not easy with no carpet to soften her tread – and fled out into the sunshine, overwhelmed by a sudden sense of relief that Esther had got back to her own time. Or at least she had to assume she had got back safely. She worried that the mirror might have taken Esther back to a different day; but then she remembered she had come back to her own time on the same day she had left. It seemed to be just if you went on a different day that time had moved on differently there.

It was nearly afternoon now, and as she walked back to the station, asking the way several times without Esther to guide her, Caroline imagined Esther being welcomed with surprise and delight by her mother and sister. They'd be sitting down to tea, probably just bread and a bit of jam, judging from what Esther had told her about how poor they were. Caroline smiled, sharing their happiness, almost feeling she was there with them, she felt so close to her teenage Gran.

The journey back was like a dream. Caroline felt only half in her own world, still half with Esther in hers.

By the time she stepped off the train, though, and

started the walk back to Stroma, she felt she was hurtling back into her own time much too fast. She remembered guiltily the cracked mirror, which she had yet to own up about. She knew how much that mirror meant to Gran – and now she knew why. But then, if that was the reason why Gran loved the mirror because of what had happened, perhaps she wouldn't be cross… ? Caroline gave up puzzling it through – it was too complicated. She would just have to say sorry.

When she got in, Caroline ran upstairs to replace the old gloves and shawl, putting off the moment when she would have to face Gran. She turned her eyes from the mirror as she ran past, not wanting to see the gaping scar in the silver.

She pulled the drawer open and pushed in the gloves and the shawl. But as she did so, her fingers knocked against something small and hard, hidden beneath the handkerchiefs at the back of the drawer. She hesitated, then groped around and closed her fist around it. She pulled it out, knowing it was something she had half expected to find. It was a small plastic doll, wearing a faded little tee shirt and shorts.

Carrying the doll with her, she set off to find Gran. She didn't have far to look. Gran was standing halfway up the stairs, beside the cracked mirror, looking up at Caroline as she came down.

The two looked at one another and then at the mirror. In the end Gran spoke. "It was you, Caroline, wasn't it?"

Caroline knew that she wasn't just talking about the crack in the mirror. Gran had at last discovered who had taken her home all those years ago – it was her own grand-daughter. That was why Gran and Esther had been unable to see each other – because they were the same person, like looking in a mirror across a lifetime.

Gran pulled Caroline to her and hugged her as if she would never stop. Then, at last, they pulled apart and looked into each other's eyes, each reflected in the other's brimming tears. Gran took Caroline's hands and noticed for the first time the tiny doll she was holding. Gran's hand closed over hers and they both laughed and held each other tight once more.

"Don't worry about the mirror, Caroline," she whispered. "It was worth it. Thank you." And then Caroline knew for sure that things had turned out all right for Esther after she had seen her disappear for the last time through the mirror.

Gran and Caroline never spoke again about what had happened. They both knew, and sharing the knowledge was enough. To talk about it would be to try and understand it, to explain it, and somehow neither of them wanted it explained or understood.

Gran never had the mirror mended, ignoring Mum and Dad's worries about the cracked glass falling from the frame. It was a reminder to her and to Caroline that however it had happened, it had happened; the crack made it real.

For two years Caroline carried on going to Gran's each summer holiday, and it was always special. As she got older she understood more about those stories Gran had told about the little presents she'd been given in service.

She understood why Gran had wanted to buy Stroma – to be the equal of those she had once served, who had even taken away her name, by owning the house they had once owned. And perhaps that one day she would be there to find out who had crossed the mirror to bring her comfort and to take her home. So that, at last, she could say thank you.

Then Gran became very ill and had to leave Stroma, and Caroline felt she did her mourning for her then, that she had already lost her. For after that

Gran was never the same person; it was very difficult for her to keep up with a conversation, and she didn't walk very well. Although Caroline visited her in hospital and later in the old people's home near their home, for the first time in her life she found it difficult to talk to her; and she missed her so much.

Gran seemed to have forgotten everything that had happened, and Caroline felt alone with the memory they had once shared.

Then, one day, Caroline's mother came home to tell her Gran had died. She and Mum hugged each other with tears in their eyes and Caroline remembered that day when she and Gran had hugged each other in the same way and the tears ran down her face onto Mum's shoulder.

Then Mum told her that before she died Gran had talked quite happily, more clearly than she had done for months. She had talked about Stroma and the mirror on the stairs…

"And something about you, Caroline, taking her home to her mother one Mothering Sunday… she must have got things mixed up, you know how she did… "

And then Caroline knew that Gran hadn't forgotten, that the memory had been locked away in her heart too, and that comforted her.

Now that Gran had died, Stroma was to be sold. Mum and Dad had to go up on the train to sort out the sale, and Caroline begged to go with them to see the house for one last time.

While Mum and Dad were out in the garden showing the estate agent round, Caroline went slowly up the stairs to the mirror. As she stood staring into the old mirror, she began to sob, remembering how she and Gran had stood here together that day. Through her tears the mirror was mistier than ever, clouding her reflection as she looked. Then through the mist she saw another face, not her own, though like it, and she felt the soft touch of a handkerchief wiping away her tears.

"Esther," she whispered. The face smiled gently at her, and then it was gone.